CW00433162

POLYGON NEW POETS

Dreams seem real,
even if they do die with
    the new daylight.

Do my days too
die with the night?

IONA LEE

Polygon

First published in Great Britain in 2018 by Polygon,
an imprint of Birlinn Limited

West Newington House
10 Newington Road
Edinburgh
EH9 1QS

ISBN 978 1 84697 461 8

Copyright © Iona Lee, 2018

All rights reserved. No part of this publication may
be reproduced, stored, or transmitted in any form, or
by any means electronic, mechanical or photocopying,
recording or otherwise, without the express written
permission of the publisher.

The moral right of Iona Lee to be identified as the author
of this work has been asserted by her in accordance
with the Copyright, Designs and Patents Act 1988.

Typeset in Verdigris MVB by Polygon
Printed by TJ International, Padstow, Cornwall

CONTENTS

ANICCA

Sometimes it is slow like
syrup off a spoon.
We bring it tea and watch
it lie there gasping.
We wrap it in tartan and
take it to a view to feel.

Sometimes it is rapid,
unreal, like a dream
dropped, lost in
unexpected consciousness.

But we all must end
so that others can exist.
That is the cost.

FORGOTTEN GODS

A withering howl quiets down –
eaten before it even ate air.

Then I am a run rabbit, run
stunned and staring
at a spyglass sun stream.

A warm amber eye like a lion's
is the hole in the sky from where we fell.
The world is the bottom of a well
and our words erupt to
nowhere, all air expelled.

We are forgotten gods.
Lost to the landscape, and
distant now like cirrus clouds.

Once we were worshipped, now our
wings are clipped, we are wind whipped
and sleeping.

On the horizon,
soon a sunrise shining on this town
where all the locals know magic.
Soon a sunrise shining down.

Our names were holy, holy,
and cherished by the tongue.
Now we are the lowly untrodden
tanglewood, the warm light and the witchcraft.

Songs once sung to praise us
erased by the winds that
wear down stone.

They don't pray to me anymore, they've
forgotten who the days were named for.

On the horizon,
soon a sunrise shining on this town
where all the locals know magic.
Soon a sunrise shining down.

So I take on the ocean
and make a mountain of myself.
Forever seeing sea spray, salt crust,
cast out and nothinged on my tongue.

Skin stung hot by the cold –
nipping pin pricks
from the dripping shale cliffs
dipped in hieroglyphic gold.

Ghostly against the
ancient night.
As dark as a lost
mind or lost eyes.

On the horizon,
soon a sunrise shining on this town
where all the locals know magic.
A sunrise will soon be shining down.

MILK IN WATER

Let it crackle in the background.

I sit
in the absence of electricity
complicit in my melancholy.

Breathe in smoke like the haar
and dim the night; ears
underwater in a warm bath.

Or the morning I woke to hear
that Hallelujah had died,
I played Famous Blue Raincoat
to the empty room and
wallowed in the news.

I hide in steam-filled showers,
a soft mollusc in his shell.
Hide till the mirror conceals me
and the moon becomes a cataract eye.

SOLITUDE

Time is terminal and we
must get on with all this living, so
I fill the space between us, and
its ancient ugliness.

I creep like a clock that ticks like
a dripping tap through each day.

I step on full-stopped forest floors and
the woodland is a thousand different corridors,
people sneak up on me from my insides.

I am happy occasionally,
when I think no one is looking.
They shiver jackets from themselves, drink
me in with the atmosphere.

I watch it all in gasps of sight from
the smudged windows of the evening
train, and a murder of crows on electricity
lines make lyrical silhouettes on the skies.

If you were a bird it would be
a cliché, like if I was a baker in a
rom-com and all of my cupcakes
were unreasonable colours.

And if you were a metaphor, you'd
probably be the moon, being
all moony in the dark that stretches out
far beyond the edges of this poem.

Somewhere in all of that my
body is a pale flame, the
tap dripping like a clock ticking.

THE FEAR

Dawn breaks like a dropped teacup
unleashing a storm that wakes me up
and I trace a trail of discarded clothes
like breadcrumbs back to a bottle.

I remember freckles on his face.
Each a speck of dust, still,
suspended in a slice of sunlight
in a white-walled space.

Now the night before is similarly scattered –
strewn confetti on the floor.

As morning sidled in they scarpered, scuttled,
scurried in a hurry out the door or
through the cracks in the floorboards, hoarding
behind wallpaper, patient, and
waiting for the night before to
do a full revolution then come back for more.

Leaving me alone in the quiet of it all
regretting cigarettes and
secrets slipped, stumbled,
tripped forth from my drunken lips
like drunkards stumbling from a bar.

SUNSHINE IN A PUDDLE

I went to the doctor to find out who she is.
He gave me some pills to help me cope.
She is difficult sometimes and
won't do what I say.

Sometimes she and I won't talk for a while,
sharing awkward silences as we wash
dishes or butter toast.

If I am in the bath, then I cannot escape
her, I cannot live in the muted glow of screen
or in his shining eyes.

She is half-innocent, half-wise.

I have staring contests with blank pieces of
paper as she watches from the corner.
She is not mighty. Perhaps,
I would find more inspiration in
me if she were so.

I want more hammering of fingernails
into empty walls or
screaming at the god-filled skies.
But she is quiet, she is damp,
heavy like sodden clothes.

Sometimes, I wish that she would just
piss off for a while,
not sit there with a scythe-like smile.
And sometimes she does, and there is
sunshine in a puddle.

But she will be there when I get back
home and I climb into
bed and we cuddle.

WET HOT HAPPINESS

I hold this poem like a cup
and pour our happiness into it.

Let it sit,
let me look at it.

You're there
running a finger
up the length
of my unshaved leg.

You giggling.

We spill wet hot happiness on
the bed, teeth touching,
white bum like a loaf of bread.

We could do this over and over,
toes holding up the blanket.
A dark tent den.

And then again and again
and over and then
it's over again.

Oh to be this safe and warm,
and this happy! This naked
and this nothing
and everything
all at once.

Oh to wake up and want
to keep on living.

GOD IS THE ONLY GHOST

God is the only ghost, haunting his creation.

The sole member of his species
all tomorrows orbiting forward
into freckled eternity.

He gulps down the days.
Sometimes he sits on the Earth's edge
and swings his feet.

Sometimes he pretends that all stones
are bald heads half-buried.
Sometimes he whispers assistance
into each side's ear.

Sundays God rests,
he blurs out the mutterings:
pleas that never stop.

God is scared to look Man in the eye.
He worries that in the dark pool of the pupil
there will be no one looking back.

Sometimes God doesn't believe in us.
He lashes out lonely, clumsy-handed,

drops plagues and weeps floods
for us to drown in.

He wonders if any of us are truly alive
or just a lie he fathomed
from the depths of his desolation.

He wonders if he'd know the difference.

His tremendous hand shook up the stars
before sending them out like so many
dice across the black baize.

They cascaded down all of forever
spinning like pennies,
spilling from pockets.

Now all in their places
the stars' dice faces
show just how well
God's bet has gone.

The things that we create
take on a life separate from ourselves.

Now Man creates God,
so he prefers to observe,
like a parent watching
as their child takes on the swings.

God sees that we too are alone
inside of ourselves.
The body is the place, he thinks,
the space we inhabit
when we all close our eyes.

Freckled eternity.

The universe will one day die with
him, or will it carry on?

IT WAS SUMMER OUTSIDE

But we were in bed,
fully dressed.
I think you still had your
shoes on.

All lazy, stoned and laughing,
we were listening to an
audiobook and laughing.

That day was fresh
like sheets
and it was new
and we were too
and we were so excited.

Because we were women
and women were cocaine,
jazz, perspective.

We were the new craze.
And there was so much still
to find out, out of
my mind on love
for that room
and that moment
and that you.

You were sitting up
talking about feminism,
slurring your slow words.

I always liked your face.
So bright
and full of mischief.
Small and blonde
and your eyes so blue
and you were so electric.

The audiobook was talking
about pubic hair,
'Do you shave down there?'

That sort of thing.
We had decided that we
didn't fucking care.

It was a revelation.
To talk about sex
and women's rights
and broken boys
and wanking.

Imagine.
It was summer outside
and we were going to change
the world.

It was summer outside
and we were cocaine
and you were electric
and I was a feminist
and your eyes were blue
and hey look mine are too.
And you were laughing.

So, we were going to move in
    together
and live like this always.
Bohemian. All cheese cloth
and opinions.

Sexy to be strident,
you said.

Manu Chao on the radio
I'd be dancing in a
dressing gown.

A waterfall of tangled hair
down my back
I'd be beautiful.
You'd be smoking on the sofa.

So it wouldn't be Paris,
but we'd pretend it was.
We'd drink whisky

with revolutionaries.
Make friends with the old
men in pubs who
had stories to tell.

We'd find new ways to
get in trouble.
Play records. Play dress up.
Fuck up. Fuck pretty people –
go on walks on Sundays.

When I wasn't working in
the bookshop or working
on this writing thing.

Because we were young women
and that was so exciting.